Kalo Li's
New Country

by Kalo Li as told to Hazel Edwards

illustrated by Coralie Islip

The Characters

Kalo Li
I moved from Hong Kong to a new country.

Mum and Dad
They run a Chinese restaurant.

The Setting

CONTENTS

Chapter 1
Life in Hong Kong 2

Chapter 2
A New Country 10

Chapter 3
School Gets Better ... 18

Chapter 4
Working at the
'Ping On' Restaurant ... 26

Chapter 5
Serving Spring Rolls .. 34

Chapter 6
The Head Teacher
Is Coming 42

Chapter 7
Saturday Night 48

CHAPTER 1

Life in Hong Kong

My name is Kalo Li. I was born in Hong Kong.

I lived in Hong Kong until I was eight. My brother and I lived with my aunt.

In Hong Kong, it is normal for children to live with other family members. We lived with my aunt so that my parents could work hard. Lots of Hong Kong families help each other like this.

My aunt has a daughter who is older than me. They're a wonderful family.

It is very expensive to live in Hong Kong. People have to work very hard.

My dad worked as a chef in a restaurant.
My mum worked in the same restaurant.
We only saw them at weekends.

I went to a Chinese school in Hong Kong. Chinese schools are very strict. Homework has to be done on time or you have to stay after school.

At the end of the year, there is a test. They put you in order from first to last.

We all spoke Chinese. We did learn a little English like, "I want to go to the toilet. I am a girl. My name is Kalo."

CHAPTER 2

A New Country

My parents came here a year before me. They needed to find somewhere to live. My dad also wanted to get a job.

They took my younger brother with them. I stayed in Hong Kong with my aunty. I was lonely without them.

Mum would phone me in Hong Kong. She would tell me how much she missed me.

Then Mum came to get me. I was eight when I left Hong Kong.

When I arrived here, Mum didn't work.
She stayed at home and looked after us.

I started going to the local school. I had trouble understanding what people said. I was teased and I cried a lot.

So I started going to a language school to learn English. At that school we practised speaking and reading English. The practice helped a lot.

I went there for half a year. I was put up a class when my English got better.

CHAPTER 3

School Gets Better

When I went back to my local school Mum said, "Go back to the lower class, just to make it easier for you."

So I did.

I like this school now. I like to make my school work look fancy and I like maths, but I still get shaky before tests.

At first, I was what you would call a "loner". I was shy and kept to myself. I didn't have many friends.

That's changed now. My two best friends are Meley, who is African and Cam-Tu who is from Vietnam.

I belong to a group of seven girls who are all friends. They invite me to their parties.

My parents are strict. I'm not allowed to go to parties at night or to sleep-overs.

Once my friend had a party on Friday night. I wasn't allowed to go.

They ordered the food for the party from our restaurant. I sent my friends a message on the take-away bag. I told them to have a good time.

CHAPTER 4

Working at the 'Ping On' Restaurant

My parents now run the 'Ping On' restaurant. The 'Ping On' restaurant had this name before we came. My parents liked the name so they kept it. 'Ping On' means safety and good luck!

The restaurant has been here for a long time. It is famous in this area. My mum is very good at talking to people. All the old customers keep coming back.

The 'Ping On' restaurant is very red. It has red walls and red chairs. Red is for good luck.

Red is also Mum's favourite colour. If you open her wardrobe, all her clothes are red!

I work at the 'Ping On' restaurant on Friday and Saturday nights.

I sometimes help Mum in the kitchen, but I don't cook. I pack the take-away food. I make the spring rolls and do jobs like that.

Most of the time I work as a waitress.
I write down what people want to eat.
I give the order to the kitchen. Then
I take the food to the table.

When I first started working in the restaurant, I was really shy. When kids my own age came to eat, I always felt they were staring at me.

Working in the restaurant has changed me. I'm more willing to talk to people. I now like to see my school friends when they come in.

CHAPTER 5

Serving Spring Rolls

For work, I wear a dark skirt, a red vest and a white shirt. My black hair is tied back with a red ribbon.

When I first started as a waitress, I dropped a few things. I practised carrying plates in the kitchen. Mum watched me.

I was very nervous when I took my first plates to a table. You need to be able to carry more than one plate and not spill anything. Finally, I got the hang of it.

The other thing I needed to learn was how to serve spring rolls. You need to pick spring rolls up with a fork and spoon. It is very difficult to do. I dropped one on a customer once.

I still have great trouble with spring rolls! They always fly everywhere.

A good thing about working in the restaurant is being able to choose any dish I like. Chow Mein is my favourite.

Some customers are funny and have a joke with you. Old people seem to be easier to talk to.

Others aren't so nice. When they order their food, they say things like, "No salt. No soy sauce. Be quick about it."

I'm very careful when taking down their order, so that I get it right.

CHAPTER

The Head Teacher Is Coming

Our school had a Food Day. Mum made me some honey king prawns to take to school.

The head teacher was very impressed with our Hong Kong food.

On Friday, the head teacher said, "We're going to visit your restaurant, Kalo. My staff and I will be coming tomorrow night for dinner".

My face went red. I wondered what the head teacher would order. What if he didn't like the food? What if I dropped a spring roll on him?

What would my head teacher say to Mum? I was not the best student in the school.

What if my teacher said something bad to Mum about my schoolwork? The teachers would probably order spring rolls too.

CHAPTER

Saturday Night

The head teacher and the other teachers came to the restaurant.

"Hello, Kalo," they said.

"Good evening," I said as my face went red. I really wanted to serve them well.

They looked at the menu.

"We'll have spring rolls first please, Kalo," said one of the teachers.

I served the spring rolls very carefully. The dish tipped but I didn't drop any.

The head teacher told Mum, "Kalo is working hard at school. I'd like to take a photo of Kalo."

He took a photo of all of us. My face was as red as the chairs in the restaurant.

"That was a wonderful meal," the head teacher said. All the teachers agreed. They even left me a tip!

On Monday the head teacher brought the photo to school. He pinned it on the board.

The teachers are coming back to the restaurant soon.

I still feel new in this country but I like being here.

GLOSSARY

aunty
Mum's sister

customers
people who buy things

expensive
costs a lot of money

head teacher
the head of a school

Hong Kong
a Chinese island city

restaurant
a shop where you sit down to eat

Vietnam
an Asian country

waitress
the person who serves you at a restaurant

Hazel Edwards

What is your favourite breakfast?
> **Toast and banana.**

Who is your favourite cartoon character?
> **The Wheelie Wonder.**

What was your least favourite activity at school?
> **Sewing.**

Why is the sky blue?
> **It depends on your viewpoint.**

Coralie Islip

What is your favourite breakfast?
> **Hot raisin toast.**

Who is your favourite cartoon character?
> **Calvin from Calvin and Hobbs.**

What was your least favourite activity at school?
> **PE and sport.**

Why is the sky blue?
> **I think blue is God's favourite colour.**